Kirsty

s

A catalogue record for this book is available from the British Library.

First edition

Published by Ladybird Books Ltd Loughborough Leicestershire UK

© 1993 The Walt Disney Company
Printed in EC

Snow White
and the Seven Dwarfs

Ladybird Books

Once upon a time, in a faraway castle, there lived a lovely little princess named Snow White.

Her vain and wicked stepmother, the Queen, feared that one day Snow White's beauty would be greater than her own. So she dressed Snow White in rags and forced her to scrub the castle floors on her hands and knees. Snow White obeyed without complaint.

The Queen had a magic mirror, which spoke to her. Every day she stood before it and demanded:

"Magic mirror, on the wall, Who is the fairest one of all?"

And every day the mirror replied:

"You, O Queen, are the fairest one of all."

This always made the vain Queen smile with pleasure.

But as Snow White grew up, the Queen began to worry. She could see that even in her rags, Snow White was becoming a beautiful young woman.

Snow White knew nothing of her stepmother's jealousy. She did her work cheerfully and when she could, she daydreamed to make her dreary life a little easier. She dreamed that one day a charming prince would arrive on a white horse and carry her off to his castle.

Then, one day, a prince *did* come riding by. Hearing Snow White singing, he climbed over the castle wall to investigate.

The Prince was so entranced by Snow White's beauty that he walked straight up to her and joined in her song.

Startled by the Prince's sudden appearance, Snow White fled up the castle steps and closed the door behind her. But then, feeling a little braver, she went out onto the balcony to wave to the handsome stranger.

The Queen, who was watching from a window, was furious.
She rushed to her mirror and cried:

"Magic mirror, on the wall,
Who is the fairest one of all?"

The mirror replied:

"Famed is thy beauty, Majesty,
But hold, a lovely maid I see,
Rags cannot hide her gentle grace,
Alas, she is more fair than thee.
Lips red as a rose, hair black as ebony,
Skin white as snow…"

"It's Snow White!" shrieked the Queen. Blazing with anger,
she summoned her huntsman. "Take Snow White to the forest,"
she ordered, "and kill her!"

The next morning the huntsman invited Snow White to go for a walk with him. Snow White was pleased to have a rest from all her work.

In the forest, the huntsman watched as Snow White happily picked wild flowers.

When Snow White's back was turned, the huntsman took out his dagger and crept up behind her. Turning suddenly, Snow White caught sight of the dagger gleaming in the sunlight. She shrank back in horror, her arms raised in defence.

Slowly, the huntsman lowered the knife. "It's no good," he cried, sinking to his knees at Snow White's feet. "I can't do it. Forgive me, Your Highness. The Queen has ordered me to kill you. Run away and hide in the forest!"

Snow White knew there was no time to lose. She thanked the huntsman for sparing her life, then ran off into the forest.

Her heart beat wildly as she rushed and stumbled through the woods. The further she ran, the darker it grew. It seemed as if even the trees were reaching out and trying to grab her.

"Where shall I go? Where shall I hide?" she cried as she fled deeper into the woods.

Faster and faster she ran, until she could run no more. Falling to the ground, she burst into tears.

She thought of her home, now so far away. And she thought of the Prince – would she ever see him again?

Just then, she heard a noise. She looked up. All around her were little blinking lights, the eyes of the friendly forest creatures.

Snow White cheered up at once. "Can you help me?" she asked. "I need somewhere to sleep. Do you know where I can go?"

The animals nodded. Then, chirping and chattering, they led her through the forest to a little cottage by a stream.

When Snow White saw the house, she clapped her hands with joy. "What a lovely cottage!" she exclaimed. "It's so small and cosy! Who lives there?"

The animals didn't answer. They just gently nudged her forwards.

She crept up to the door and knocked. There was no answer. "Perhaps I'll just peep inside," she said, opening the door.

Everything inside the house was tiny.

"Oh, my!" said Snow White, "the children who live here must have no mother to look after them. Look at all the dust and cobwebs! Now that I'm here, perhaps I'll just tidy up a bit."

Soon not only Snow White, but all the animals, too, were busy dusting and sweeping. A rabbit held the dustpan for Snow White, and two squirrels unravelled cobwebs and dusted the shelves with their tails.

When everything downstairs was neat and clean, Snow White decided to have a look upstairs.

Holding a candle, Snow White followed her friends up the stairs. There she found seven small beds, all lined up in a row. A name was carved on each one: *Happy, Dopey, Grumpy, Sneezy, Sleepy, Bashful* and *Doc*.

"What funny names these children have!" said Snow White. Suddenly she yawned. "Sleepy... I'm feeling a bit sleepy myself. Perhaps I'll have a little nap..." She lay down on one of the beds, and before she could say another word, she was fast asleep.

The animals crept out quietly, leaving the tired Princess to rest.

Meanwhile, in a nearby mine, seven little men were finishing their day's work. They were the dwarfs who lived in the little house in the forest.

Every morning at dawn, the dwarfs left their home to go and search for diamonds in a tunnel that they had dug deep inside a mountain. They sang as they worked:

"We dig, dig, dig, dig, dig, dig, dig,
From early morn till night.
We dig, dig, dig, dig, dig, dig,
Up everything in sight!"

Now it was time to stop their work and set off for home.

Carrying their pickaxes on their shoulders, the dwarfs
marched through the forest in a line.

"Heigh-ho! Heigh-ho! It's home from work we go," they sang.

Doc, holding a lantern, led the way. Behind him was Grumpy,
then Happy, Sleepy, Sneezy, Bashful and last of all, Dopey. The
seven tired and hungry dwarfs were looking forward to reaching
their snug little home.

Suddenly Doc stopped in his tracks.

"Whaa-whaaaa-what's AAAHH-CHOOO! wrong?" asked Sneezy.

"Look!" said Doc, pointing towards the house. "There's a light in the window!"

"Oh, no! Someone must be inside!" squeaked Bashful in his tiny voice.

"I'm tired. Let's go in," said Sleepy with a yawn.

"Careful, men!" whispered Grumpy. "It might be a robber!"

The dwarfs tiptoed up to the house and slowly pushed the door open, taking care not to make a sound. All seven of them peered round the door at once.

They were speechless. Never had they seen their home looking so spotless. They could hardly believe their eyes.

"Gosh," said Bashful, "our cobwebs are missing!"

"Someone's stolen our dishes," said Sneezy, looking in the empty sink.

"They're not stolen!" said Happy. "They've been hidden in the cupboard."

"Humph!" said Grumpy. "We'd better find the person who did this."

"Let's look upstairs," said Sleepy, who was worried about his bed.

The dwarfs crept up the stairs, ready for battle. As they entered the bedroom, they saw a large shape sprawled across their beds.

"Quick, let's kill it before it wakes up!" said Grumpy.

The dwarfs moved closer to the bed, their pickaxes ready to strike.

"Ssssh!" whispered Doc. "It's moving!"

At once, all seven dwarfs ran and hid at the foot of the beds.

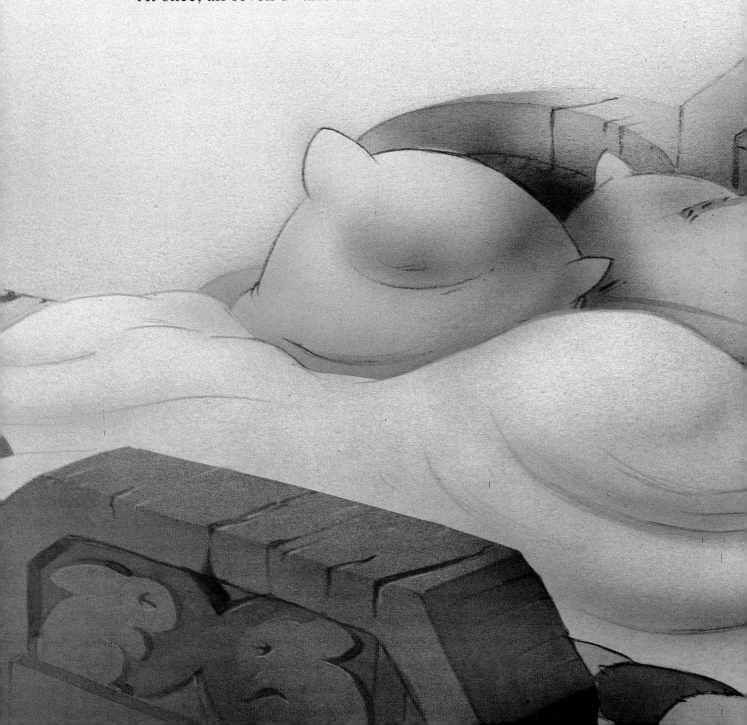

Sure enough, the large shape was moving. It stretched out its arms and yawned.

The dwarfs kept still. No one dared to move a muscle.

But Sneezy couldn't control himself. "AH-AHH-AAAHHH-CHOOO!" His enormous sneeze was enough to wake anyone.

And that's exactly what happened. Snow White sat up and came out from under the sheets.

Happy was the first to speak. "A girl!" he said, beginning to laugh. "Our robber is a girl!"

Snow White began to giggle, too. "Why, you're little men. And I thought you were children!" she said. *Everyone* began to laugh at that. Everyone, that is, except Grumpy, who scowled in the background.

Snow White told the dwarfs who she was and how she had come to their house. The dwarfs felt sorry for her when they heard what her wicked stepmother had done.

"Don't worry, Snow White," said Doc. "You can stay here with us. We'll protect you from the wicked Queen."

"Not so fast!" said Grumpy. "We should think about this."

"There's nothing to think about," said Doc. "The Princess will stay with us!"

"Hurrah!" shouted the dwarfs, flinging their caps in the air.

Meanwhile, in her room in the castle, the Queen looked into her mirror and asked:

"Magic mirror, on the wall,
Who now is the fairest one
of all?"

The mirror replied:

"Over the seven jewelled hills,
Beyond the seventh fall,
In the cottage of the seven
dwarfs,
Dwells Snow White,
The fairest one of all."

"Snow White lies dead in the forest," said the Queen. "The huntsman has brought me proof." She opened the lid of a small box and held it up to the mirror. "Look, her heart."

But the mirror replied:

"Snow White still lives –
The fairest in the land,
'Tis the heart of a pig
You hold in your hand."

"I've been tricked!" screamed the Queen, throwing the box to the floor.

Enraged, the Queen ran down the steps leading to a secret room in the castle's deepest dungeon. There she prepared a magic potion to change her appearance so that Snow White would not recognise her.

"I'll trick her just as I've been tricked!" she said to the raven who watched from above.

The potion worked! In an instant, the Queen was transformed into an ugly old woman.

"Ha, ha, ha!" she cackled. "Now, my little Snow White, I'm going to prepare a special treat just for you!" She took a plump red apple and plunged it into a cauldron filled with boiling poison.

"One bite of this apple and she'll be dead," hissed the wicked Queen. "*Then* we'll see who is the most beautiful woman in the kingdom!"

It was dinner time at the dwarfs' house. Seven hungry little men rushed towards the table.

"Wait a minute," said Snow White. "First show me your hands."

"I knew there'd be trouble," mumbled Grumpy, as the dwarfs looked at one another in surprise.

"Now, now," said Snow White softly, "let me see your hands."

One by one, the dwarfs held out their hands.

"Oh, my goodness, this will never do! Look at those grubby hands and dirty fingernails!" said Snow White. "No one comes to the table with hands like those. Go and wash or you won't get anything to eat!" she said, pointing to the water trough outside.

All the dwarfs obediently went out and began to wash – all, that is, except Grumpy.

"Now look what she's done," he muttered. "I'd like to see anyone make me wash if I didn't want to."

He was so busy grumbling that he didn't notice the other dwarfs sneak up on him until it was too late. They dragged him to the trough and scrubbed him till he shone.

After dinner, the dwarfs
decided to have a party for their
princess. They brought out their
musical instruments, and took
turns dancing with Snow White.

Dopey wanted to surprise Snow White. He wrapped himself in a long coat and climbed onto Sneezy's shoulders. Now he was as tall as the Princess!

"Why, who's this dashing young man?" asked Snow White, as she began dancing with him. It all went well until Sneezy let out an enormous ATISHOO! and Dopey and Sneezy collapsed in a heap.

That night, while Snow White and the dwarfs slept peacefully in their beds, the wicked Queen left the castle by way of the moat that separated it from the forest. An evil gleam flashed in her eyes as she rowed towards the forest's edge. A basket of shiny red apples lay at her feet.

The next morning, the dwarfs lined up for inspection before setting off for work. Snow White made sure their hands and faces were clean, and she rewarded each dwarf with a kiss.

"Now, remember," warned Doc, "the Queen is full of witchcraft, so beware of strangers!"

"Don't worry," said Snow White. "I'll be all right."

When the dwarfs had gone, Snow White began to prepare a special treat for them. "I'm going to bake a pie," she told her animal friends, who had come to visit.

Suddenly she heard footsteps approaching. "Who can that be?" wondered Snow White.

A ragged old woman appeared at the window. She offered Snow White some rosy red apples to put in the pie she was making.

The birds twittered in alarm. They knew that the old woman was really the Queen in disguise. Fluttering and squawking, they dived at the Queen, knocking the apple from her hand.

Snow White ran outside, waving her arms to chase the birds away. "Shame on you for frightening the poor old woman," she scolded.

The kind Princess helped the old lady to her feet and took her inside for a drink of water.

The animals gathered outside the window and looked on in horror as Snow White took one of the apples. They heard the wicked Queen say, "It's a magic wishing apple. One bite and all your dreams will come true."

Realising that it was a trick, the animals raced off to find the dwarfs.

The animals pulled and tugged at the dwarfs' clothing, desperately trying to warn them of the danger Snow White was in.

Sneezy was the one who realised what was wrong. "Perhaps the Queen has got Snow White," he said.

"Snow White!" gasped Grumpy. "We've got to save her!"

But it was too late.

As soon as Snow White had bitten into the apple, she had fallen to the floor as if she were dead.

The wicked Queen cackled with glee. "Only love's first kiss can save you now, my pretty little princess!" Her evil laugh echoed through the little house.

"Now I will return to the castle," said the Queen. "My magic mirror will tell me the truth. *Now* we'll see who's the fairest one of all!" And she rushed out into the forest.

The dwarfs sped towards their house, riding on the backs of the deer.

"There she is!" cried Grumpy. "After her!"

When she saw the dwarfs, the Queen fled in the opposite direction. The dwarfs followed, waving sticks and pickaxes.

The sky darkened, and rain began to fall.

The Queen climbed to the
top of a cliff. "I'm trapped!" she
cried. Then she had an idea. She
picked up a stick and used it to
try to loosen a huge boulder.
Grumpy was the first to spot
her.

"Look out!" he warned the
others. "She's trying to crush us
with that boulder!"

Thunder rumbled, and rain
pelted down from the sky.

The enormous stone began to move.
Then a loud crack of thunder sounded, and
a tremendous bolt of lightning split the air.
Startled by the noise, the Queen lost her
balance and fell backwards into the
darkness.

When the next flash of lightning lit up the
sky, the boulder was still there. But the
wicked Queen had disappeared for ever.

When the weary dwarfs returned to their house, they found Snow White lying on the floor. They lifted her up and gently put her on her bed. Tears streamed down their faces as they knelt beside their beloved princess.

The dwarfs could not bear to bury Snow White. They made a special coffin for her out of the clearest crystal, so that they could always see her lovely face.

They put the coffin in the middle of the forest, where all her animal friends could see her. Day after day the dwarfs visited her, each one wishing with all his heart that she would wake up.

When spring arrived, flowers blossomed around Snow White's tomb.

One day, as the dwarfs knelt in the forest, they heard the sound of hoofbeats. They looked up and saw a handsome young man riding up on a white horse. It was Snow White's true love!

The Prince jumped off his horse and ran to the coffin. Slowly, he lifted the crystal lid.

"I've found you at last!" whispered the Prince. Leaning towards Snow White, he gently kissed her pale lips.

Suddenly Snow White's eyelids began to flutter. A smile spread slowly across her face. She opened her eyes.

Snow White was alive!

Shouts of joy rang out as the Prince gathered Snow White into his arms and lifted her onto his horse. The dwarfs danced around and hugged one another with delight.

Snow White looked down at her friends. "Goodbye," she called as the Prince led her away to his castle high on a hill.

And so Snow White's dearest wish came true, for she and her prince lived happily ever after.